MW01143845

Ferry Tales

Wit, wisdom, and a bartenders' secrets

from the bar of the Port Jefferson Ferry

By

Bob Sciascia

Cover art by Dennis Coburn

To my wife Cookie, who never stopped believing in my dreams and kept me from being lost in the clouds, who halves my sorrows and doubles my joys. I love you. Bob.

Ferry Tales...an Introduction

A ferry ride is a kind of time out. When you get on the boat there's nothing you can do until you get to the other side. So ferries tend to be places where people relax and let their hair down.

This is a book by and about the people who ride the ferry across Long Island Sound between Port Jefferson, Long Island and Bridgeport, Connecticut. The ferry service was started in 1883 as a way to save interstate travelers a long detour through New York City. Today three big car ferries make the sixteen-mile trip thirty times a day in all weathers, carrying a million passengers a year.

Many of these passengers head straight for the bar. The crossing takes only about an hour, and this is a convivial time. Some passengers are regular commuters; others are on vacation, or heading to or from sports events or casinos. They all meet to relax in the bar, which is right at the front of the ferry under the bridge, with a fine panoramic view of the ocean.

Behind the bar stands Bob the barman. That's me. I've been tending bar on this ferry for thirteen years, and it gets more interesting all the time. I meet people from every walk of life, and they seem to open up on the ferry. Perhaps it's my engaging personality, or perhaps it's the alcohol, but over the years I've heard a lot of stories that are both enlightening and inspiring, and a lot of others that are just plain funny.

I wanted to capture some of these brief encounters to share with others, so I placed some notebooks on the bar. Each notebook had printed on the front in large black letters, **This is What I Know to Be True**. Everyone was invited to add something, and they did.

The floodgates opened, and the books soon filled up with quotations, aphorisms, stories, and jokes from people at the bar. This book is a selection of the best (and most legible!) comments from the first five notebooks, and I hope you enjoy reading them as much as I have enjoyed connecting with these people and sharing these moments in their lives.

I would like to acknowledge the cooperation and support of the Bridgeport and Port Jefferson Steamboat Company, my employer Frank Marino, Cathy Lee Gibson who helped put the material together, our editor Linda LiDestri who made sense of it all, my on-board friend David Bouchier who organized the publication process, and all the ferry passengers who have so enriched my life and made this book possible.

The thoughts in this book come from just one bar in just one ferry, but they are so universal that they could be from any ferry in the world. I've added a whole lot of my favorite drink recipes, bar trivia, and curious facts to complete this compendium of wit and wisdom from the ferry bar. Enjoy the ride.

Bob Sciascia
Long Island, 2005

Ferry Tales

Ferry Boat Wisdom

You can't always believe what you hear, but you can always believe your bartender. (John—48)

¤

Starting this book was smart. It gives perception and a realism that only someone with a unique job such as this could find. He cares enough to listen to what you say and write, and those who read this share the one thing in life that is the most expensive, the most valuable, and the least realized: their time.
(Woman—22)

¤

Bob, you have brought a gift of wisdom and humor to a world of strangers. Each of us should contribute as much. (Michael—55)

Barroom Basics

What are *Well*, *Call*, and *Top Shelf* Liquors?

Well is the least expensive house liquor. It's usually a brand name you've never heard of, and it's what you're going to get unless you ask for a call or a top shelf. Well liquor is what you can call a cheap shot.

Call is the next step up from well, where the popular name brands stand. You'll probably recognize these examples: Absolut, Jack Daniels, Dewers, and so on. When ordering a call drink, say, "Absolut and cranberry" instead of vodka and cranberry. The drink will cost a bit more, but it's worth it.

Top Shelf is the more expensive call. Examples are Hennessy, Glenlivet, and Courvoisier.

Premium is the most expensive top shelf liquor. Examples of premium liquors are Patron and Remy Martin. These are reserved for the connoisseur.

Good luck on your life's dream with this book... By the way, I'll have another Bud, I've dreamed about it all day. (Man—50)

¤

Lao-Tse said: "He who professes wisdom must tell others about it." This book is a tribute to that message. (Steve—51)

¤

Always tip your bartender! (Jeff—21)

¤

Don't rock the boat; it annoys the bartender. (Art—60)

Friendly Advice for Newbies

For you folks just turning 21 and for those who don't normally spend much time in bars, I would like to offer some information you may use as a guideline of acceptable bar behavior. I hope you will find this advice useful, or at very least, entertaining.

You Want Booze? Have Your I.D.

When asked for your I.D., don't give the doorman or the bartender a hard time. It doesn't matter how old you are, you must present valid I.D. in order to consume alcohol. "You're kidding me" or "How old do I look?" are not the right things to say or ask. Simply put: The law requires age verification. In addition, it is illegal to remove from the premises any drink with alcohol. And bartenders cannot and will not serve anyone who is visibly intoxicated.

The voyage across the Sound, which I've taken countless times, used to be so exciting since it meant I was leaving home and going on some sort of adventure. Now, I am far more excited for the trips going the opposite way... nothing's better than a homecoming. (Hollie—25)

¤

This boat is rockin'. I miss my family while on this trip but really enjoyed this book. (Robert—30)

¤

My biggest fear is the ocean! But I love the ferry ride. Someday, I'll overcome my fear. I know I will. I'm on my way to some R and R and I can't wait. Always believe in your dreams! Peace out. (Lisa—37)

¤

It's come to that time of the voyage to think of how lucky we are to live in this wonderful country and to have fellowship here in this bar! (Skip—56)

12

Ordering from the Bartender

When you want the bartender's attention, don't snap your fingers, don't whistle, and don't yell, "YO!" Sit or stand at the bar with your money in your hand and wait for eye contact from your bartender. He'll know what you want. Order your booze first, mixer second. Examples: Scotch and water, gin and tonic, rye and ginger ale, rum and coke, and so on. And don't say, "Scotch and water. Make it strong." If you want a double, ask for it, and be prepared to pay for it.

I'm sitting on this ferry. My car is stuck out in the lot. If I didn't have bad luck, I wouldn't have any luck at all, is what Captain Ed just said to me. But why worry, one step forward two steps back, eventually you will get there. A positive attitude is all you need. (Holly—28)

⌀

Bob the bartender says he hates when it's rough— he doesn't know who to cut off. (Jeannine—32)

⌀

Rich or poor—it's good to have money! Take the ferry, don't drive. Peace to all. Good will toward men! (Anon.)

⌀

It's not the size of the ship that makes you sick, it's the motion of the ocean. (Sheila—52)

Decisions, Decisions

Know what you want when the bartender approaches. If the bar is busy, he is going to want your drink order—fast. Questions like "What's a good drink?" or "What kind of beer do you have?" are silly and time consuming when the bar is hopping. The selection of beer and drinks is huge. If you're not sure what you want, ask to review the separate menu of beer, wine, and drinks most bars have. Later, when you are ready for another drink, just put your empty glass in front of your beverage napkin or coaster. This is a cue for any experienced bartender that you are ready for another drink without him asking you.

There is something very special and soothing about the ocean and even Long Island Sound! (Woman—46)

¤

Life is good, the food was good, I sure hope the ride is good. (Robbie—32)

¤

There's nothing better than being on the Port Jeff Ferry, heading home to Port Jeff. (Bob—44)

¤

On a ferry, never drive off the way you drove on. (Jeff—45)

¤

Enjoy life! This could be your last ferry! Be Happy! (Melissa—46)

Cash Business

Paying for a single drink with a credit card is bad bar etiquette. If you have no cash, start a tab. If you are ordering at the bar, have your cash ready.

Tipping Your Bartender

Tipping is how a bartender makes his living. Most people fall into the 15 to 20 percent range. Some people tip between 30 and 50 percent. A bartender will always treat a good tipper better than a poor tipper. If you hear your tip hit the bar, chances are you're not going to get a buy back (free drink) any time soon.

Fighting Greenhorns

Listen up, boys: If a stranger is hitting on your girlfriend, take it as a compliment and move along. If someone bumps into you or spills their drink on you, be cool and just let it be. If a customer is annoying you, tell the bartender or staff and let them take care of the problem. Have a good time and lighten up.

It's always a pleasure to ride across the Sound.
Driving is OK, but traffic hampers quality time.
(Man—55)

¤

Southern redneck has been "citified." Had a good
time on board. (Fred—35)

¤

Life's a ferry—just ride it. (Dave—29)

¤

"My life is a hobby!" Your friendly bartender
(from Port Jefferson)

¤

We are on our way to a sad family occasion. This
book brightened our day. Thank you!
(three women—53, 34, 29)

18

Don't Over Drink

Pace your drinks; few things are as embarrassing as being cut off at your favorite bar. If you feel you've had enough, do everyone a favor and cut yourself off before you get stupid.

Don't Drink and Drive

If you do not have a designated driver and you feel as if you have had too much to drink, tell your bartender. He or she will gladly call you a taxi. Remember, a cab ride is much cheaper than a DUI. It's just the right thing to do, and in the end, you just may save someone's life.

To Bob on the one millionth crossing with John and Rita from Long Island: Love one another. Treat others the way you want to be treated. Affirm your children every day. Spend time alone with your husband. It's the best. And always, always, always remember the Vietnam Vets!! (Anon.)

¤

Coming from an Irish wake...we just love the ferry. Thanks Tommy, Bob, Bob, Bob, and Richie. (Deidre, 38; Tom, 39; Erin, 35; and Siobhan, 32)

¤

Rumbling swaying craft
Sleeping talking staring, noise
of the crowd deafens
otherwise peaceful waters;
strangers are thrown together
with yelping dogs, a woman
minds my business
while a small child
smiles at me.
(Keith—34)

Raising the Bar

If you keep a bottle of each of the spirits mentioned here, you'll be able to create nearly any combination of drinks that should satisfy just about everybody.

Gin
Vodka
Rum (light and dark)
Bourbon
Scotch
Vermouth (sweet and dry)
Red and white wine (dry)
Brandy, Port, Sherry
Any assortment of liqueurs popular in your crowd

Choose a selection of mixers from the following:

It's too damn cold here. (Scott—41)

ᵡ

Ferries are cold. Thank God for the lounge.
(Woman—28)

ᵡ

This book of life experiences and philosophies is
enjoyable and enlightening to both my spirit and my
mind, which contribute to my total well being of
joy, peace, and love. Thank you. (Juanita—40)

ᵡ

The voyage was smooth, Long Island is great. But
I still hate the Yankees, Go, Boston. (Anon.)

ᵡ

On a ferry the ride is nice, the whiskey smooth,
the company pleasant. (Scott—24)

Mixers

Mineral Water
Cola
Ginger ale
Club soda or seltzer
Tonic or quinine water
Lemon-lime soda
Fresh fruit juice, especially: orange, cranberry,
grapefruit, lemon, lime.
Other juices: tomato, pineapple
Water (in a small pitcher)

Garnish

Jar of olives
Lemons
Limes
Oranges
Tabasco pepper sauce
Worcestershire sauce
Horseradish
Maraschino cherries
Coarse salt

23

Bob the bartender makes one hell of a "fluff" (vodka + Coke)!! (Jay—25)

✗

The rocking of the boat feels good when you get a couple beers in you. Makes me think of how nice it is to go home by boat, and I smile when I think about how much I'll miss it in the future, when I ride no more. (Ray—24)

✗

I must have been here a while... the whole bar is moving! (Pat—25)

✗

I truly know my drinking limit, but I am always drunk before I reach it. (Bob—52)

✗

I'm not so think as you drunk I am. (John-31)

Bar Equipment

The right tools make the job easier. For your bar at home, you'll need to have handy:

1.   Can and bottle openers
2.   Easy-to-use corkscrew
3.   Waiter's corkscrew
4.   Glass stirring rod or long spoon
5.   Coil-rimmed bar strainer
6.   A tall, heavy-duty mixing glass or shaker
7.   Small, sharp paring knife for cutting fruit or for shearing off rind
8.   Wooden muddler to mash herbs, fruit, etc.
9.   Large pitcher
10.   A jigger measure with an easy-to-read half
11.   Ice bucket and ice tongs

Electric blender (optional)
           Glassware (see pages 26 & 28)

One of my favorite toasts: Here's champagne to our real friends and real pain to our sham friends. (Mike—53)

¤

Warning: Consumption of alcohol may lead you to believe that ex-lovers are really dying for you to telephone them (or knock on their door) at four in the morning. (Man—52)

¤

The problem drinker is the one who never buys a round. (Gary—42)

¤

A bartender is just a pharmacist with a limited inventory. (Man—52)

¤

Reality is an illusion created by alcohol deficiency. (Man—52)

Measure Twice, Pour Once

You want to make a perfect drink each time?
Measure all ingredients. Remember, drinks can be
spoiled by being either too strong or too weak.

Some standard bar measures:

1 teaspoon (bar spoon)	$\frac{1}{8}$ ounce
1 dash (or splash) 1/6 teaspoon (1/32 ounce)	
1 tablespoon	$\frac{3}{8}$ ounce
1 pony	1 ounce
1 jigger (bar glass)	$1\frac{1}{2}$ ounces
1 wine glass	4 ounces
1 split	6 ounces
1 cup	8 ounces

Alcohol kills slowly—so what? Who's in a hurry?
—Robert Benchley (Anon.)

¤

I only drink to make other people more interesting.
—George Jean Nathan (Dick—56)

¤

Work is the curse of the drinking class. —Oscar
Wilde (Anon.)

¤

What soberness conceals drunkenness reveals.
(Hal—24)

¤

You've never had too much to drink until you have
to hold onto the grass to keep from falling off the
earth. (Kingfish—26)

The Right Glass for Your Drink

Highball Glass (10–12 oz.): Use for highballs, soda, and beer.

Rocks or Old-Fashioned Glass (6–10 oz.): Spirits over ice, cocktails over ice, specials like the Mai Tai and Old-Fashioned.

All-Purpose Wine Glass (8–10 oz.): Use for red or white wine and frozen drinks. Note that wine glasses are not often filled above the halfway mark.)

Shot Glass or Shooter ($\frac{3}{4}$–1 oz.): Guess we don't really have to explain this one. Might buy a few extra of these, people tend to get a bit rowdy after continual use.

Collins Glass (10–12 oz.):

Martini Glass (5–7 oz.): Use for all "up" cocktails.

London Dock or Port Glass (5–7 oz.): For port, sauternes, fine spirits, and liqueurs neat.

It's happy hour somewhere. (Anon.)

¤

Keep the Captain Morgan flowing... Drive safe...
Hugs + kisses... (Woman—32)

¤

Hold onto your drinks... It's going to be a bumpy
ride. (Michelle—31)

¤

He's a terrific drinker. All day. The potting shed's
full of his empties. He says they're for weed killer
but he's got enough there to defoliate the whole of
Suffolk. — Alan Ayckbourn (Anon.)

¤

Mona Lisa cocktail—two of them and you can't get
that silly grin off your face.
—Anonymous

Champagne Flute (4–5 oz.): Champagne and champagne cocktails.

Punch Bowl and Cups: A must if you want to start or have a holiday punch tradition.

Beer Mug: For beer or beer-shot combinations.

Beer Pilsner: Tall beer glass tapered at the bottom. Also works well for serving larger margaritas and the like.

Irish Coffee Glass (6–8 oz.): For all your warm, winter drinks.

Brandy Snifter: Oversized balloon glass with a narrow opening to the aroma.

White Wine Glass: A bit smaller than a red wine glass, with a more tulip-shaped bowl.

A cask of wine works more miracles than a church full of saints. —Italian Proverb (Anon.)

¤

"Alcohol is a very necessary article….It enables Parliament to do things at eleven at night that no sane person would do at eleven in the morning." —George Bernard Shaw (Anon.)

¤

Let's get out of these wet clothes and into a dry martini. (Anon.)

¤

If you drink, don't drive. Don't even putt. —Dean Martin (Anon.)

Knockout Punch

Punches are the way to go when serving a large number of guests. Your friends can help themselves, and since most punches are made with a single spirit, they're inexpensive and easy to prepare. Here's a recipe I used for a punch at a barbecue. Aside from hosting guests I love, it was the punch that made this party special.

Southern Comfort Punch

1 (4/5) quart bottle Southern Comfort
6 ounces fresh lemon juice
Lemonade
1 (6 oz.) can frozen orange juice
3 quarts lemon-lime soda, chilled
Red food coloring (optional)
Lemon slices (optional)
Orange slices (optional)

In a punch bowl, combine Southern Comfort, lemon juice, lemonade, and orange juice, mixing well. Add carbonated lemon-lime beverage. Add ice cubes or a block of ice, and a few drops of red food coloring, if desired. Garnish with lemon and orange slices. Serves 12–15.

I have some things to share, whether they are true, I don't know, but at least I'm sharing my experiences with you.

Friends—real friends—are hard to come by. The people who may say they are your friends may screw you in the end. It is very important to surround yourself with the right people and to make sure you stay true to these people. The true friends are <u>real</u> friends. Be real, and if you are going to be fake, then you are just confusing the important people, including yourself. If you aren't up front and real, in the long run, you are only screwing yourself. You will ruin what you have and lose what you could have received.

So if you learn anything in my words, to maintain happiness, be real to yourself and your friends (your real, true friends).

I may not be too old, but I think I know this to be true. (Joe—21)

¤

A friend's eye is a good mirror. (Pete—52)

Hiccups Cure

On many occasions when I was behind the bar, I offered 2 ounces of sour mix, 5 drops of bitters, and 1 teaspoon of sugar in an old-fashioned glass to cure hiccups. Remarkably, it worked most of the time. Try it.

A bitters-soaked lemon wedge dipped in sugar to bite into also works well.

Bean Counting

Never use an even number of coffee beans when serving Sambuca-Romana: It's considered bad luck by superstitious people. An even number of beans supposedly proves disastrous for lovers, presumably sipping from the same glass.

Numbing myself was easy. Sobering up was difficult. Being myself in every situation—without drugs or alcohol—has been enlightening. Life is beautiful, don't waste it getting wasted. (Kathy—28)

¤

Best friends are only temporary... true friends are forever. (Andy—53)

¤

A true friend always leaves us better than he finds us. (Woman—31)

¤

Wonderful holiday in New England. The foliage in the fall is awesome. Lovely to spend time with friends and relations. (Anne—60)

¤

I don't trust him. We're friends.   —Bertolt Brecht

Bloody Mary and Big Ralph

There are so many different recipes for a Bloody Mary. Every weekend bartender in the U.S.A. has his own. And of course, his is the best recipe. (But mine is really the best.)

1½ oz. vodka
3 dashes of Worcestershire sauce
4 dashes of Tabasco pepper sauce
Pinch each of salt, pepper, and celery salt
1 bar spoon of horseradish
¼ oz. fresh lemon juice
4 oz. tomato juice

Combine all the ingredients in a mixing glass and roll back and forth to mix. Strain into large goblet or pint glass three-quarters filled with ice. Garnish with lemon or lime or celery stalk.

If you use gin with this Bloody Mary mix, it's called a Red Snapper. I know this because when I was a young guy just starting out in the bar business, a customer asked for a Red Snapper. I had no idea what it was, and I was very embarrassed.

We cannot tell the precise moment when friendship is formed. As in filling a vessel, there is at last a drop that makes it run over; so in a series of kindnesses there is at least one kindness or deed that makes the heart run over. (Amy—25)

¤

I believe that friends are quiet angels who lift us to our feet when our wings have trouble remembering how to fly. (Woman—22)

¤

Forty-two years old, three kids, living in Newtown. What I know to be true is that life is composed of little moments. Sitting here today with good friends is one of those. (Dawn—42)

¤

The only pure love is that from your mother and your dog—and if you're really lucky, a sister. (Mike—39)

The funny thing is that I've been waiting 38 years now for someone, anyone, to come into my bar and ask me for a RED SNAPPER.

Big Ralph was a regular at one of the clubs I used to work in. He was a big, warm-hearted and generous man. We became fast friends. One night, Ralph walked into the club on a very busy night. Tito Puente and his 26-piece orchestra were playing. For some reason, Big Ralph didn't even notice. Before he was settled at his usual spot at the bar, I had his Bacardi and Coke waiting for him. He took a sip of his drink and said to me, "The band sounds good. Buy them a drink." "Ralph," I said, "That's a 27-piece Latin band." He said, "Buy them 27 rum and Cokes." And that's what I did. And that's Big Ralph. You gotta love him.

Today is a good day. Thank you for surrounding me with the ones I love and the ones who love me.
(Russ—30)

¤

Where there is love, there can be no sin.
(Lois—44)

¤

If you truly love someone, it does not matter how far apart you are. You will travel the distance.
(Woman—29)

¤

Love: A temporary insanity curable by marriage.
—Ambrose Bierce

Never use canned whipped cream in an Irish Coffee; whip your own cream without sugar. First, place a stainless-steel bowl or pitcher in the fridge until it is very cold. Then whisk or whip very cold heavy cream to just under stiff. The cream should have no bubbles and pour slowly.

Dubonnet Cocktail
1½ oz. Red Dubonnet
1½ oz. gin
Flaming orange twist

Pour the Dubonnet and gin together over ice in an old-fashioned glass, or chill and serve up in a cocktail (martini) glass. Garnish with flaming orange.

Don't fall in love with anyone who treats his mother badly. (Woman—54)

¤

Infinite love is an incredible thing!! (Ken—47)

¤

Love is like playing piano, first you must learn the rules, and then you must forget the rules and play with your heart. (Woman—32)

¤

Another bride, another June,
Another sunny honeymoon,
Another season, another reason,
For makin' whoopee!
—Gus Kahn

Long Island Iced Tea

Credit for this incredibly successful drink is attributed to Robert C. Butt.

1 part vodka
1 part tequila
1 part rum
1 part gin
1 part Triple Sec
1 ½ part sour mix
1 part Coca-Cola
Lemon slice

Mix ingredients together over ice in a glass. Pour into shaker and give one brisk shake. Pour back into glass and make sure there is a touch of fizz at the top. Garnish with lemon.

There are those people who live their lives and never know what it is to love. Those who are scared to say "I love you" because they feel there is nothing more after that. What you need to know is that to love is the beginning of life not the end. (Woman—31)

¤

To love is good! (Anon.)

¤

Immature love says, "I love you because I need you." Mature love says, "I need you because I love you." —Erich Fromm

¤

I believe in soul mates; mine is sitting to my left! (Anon.)

Golden Cadillac
1 oz. Galliano
1 oz. white Crème de Cacao
2 oz. heavy cream
Cinnamon

Shake with ice and strain into a chilled cocktail glass. Dust with cinnamon.

Grasshopper
1 oz. green Crème de Menthe
1 oz. White crème de Cacao
2 oz. heavy cream

Shake with ice and strain into a cocktail glass.

Thanks to the Port Jeff Ferry, I am able to be with the man I love and visit my family in New England with ease! Hello, Long Island! Good-bye Boston! (Donna—28)

¤

Who knows? My true love may be on the next ferry. (Anon.)

¤

Holding hands at midnight
'Neath a starry sky...
Nice work if you can get it,
And you can get it if you try.
—Ira Gershwin

¤

I just left my baby doll. We had a great weekend. We met in Newport and fell in love! Totally wasn't expecting that! So my advice is to enjoy today and never stop wondering about tomorrow. (Man—36)

Popping the Cork

A champagne cork can come out of a bottle with enough force to break your nose. Remove the cork with CARE.

First remove the wire around the cork. Remember that champagne bottles are loaded weapons and should be pointed in a safe direction (away from your guests). Hold the bottle at a 45 degree angle. Keep your hand over the cork at all times. Hold the cork in place with one hand while you gently twist the bottle with the other. The cork should be released slowly and should not come off with a loud pop, as we are led to believe. The mark of a successful champagne opening is a mere burp of the cork.

Your next romance may be sitting next to you.
(Anon.)

¤

I am in love! (Walter—40)

¤

To my wife:
If the sky was a sheet of paper and the ocean was
the ink to write, it wouldn't be enough to tell you
how much I love you. (Richie—64)

¤

The broken dates,
The endless waits,
The lovely loving and the hateful hates,
The conversation and the flying plates—
I wish I were in love again.
—Dorothy Parker

Mimosa
4 oz. champagne
2 oz. orange juice
Dash of Triple Sec or Cointreau

Pour the orange juice into a champagne glass and fill with the champagne. Float the Triple Sec over the drink surface.

Champagne Cocktail
Champagne
Sugar cube soaked with Angostura bitters
Lemon peel

Place the sugar cube in bottom of a champagne glass and fill the glass with champagne. Garnish with lemon peel, if desired.

I am a 32-year-old woman who just got accepted to school. I am sitting here on the ferry with my girlfriend, and I am so happy. I wonder how many people in the lounge think that we are gay. I wonder how many approve or hate it. My point is to let you all know that LOVE IS REAL—no matter the race or sexual preference. Life is too short to be unhappy. We all need to accept each other and our happiness. Good luck on your own journey to find true love and happiness—I have found it and couldn't be happier! (Woman—32)

¤

I am not one of those women who needs a man to be there 24/7. I can live by myself and enjoy it. My husband is my best friend, my lover, my true other half. He completes me (to quote Jerry Maguire). Life is good, he makes it great. So as I sit here on this ferry heading home, while he stays on the Island for a week, I'll miss him, but I'll also enjoy my week. But there's nothing like being reunited!!!
I love you Richie! Can't wait till Friday!
(Krista—29)

Mud in Your Eye

The word *toast* originates from the Latin *tostare,* which means "to burn." In Ancient Rome, a piece of toasted bread was dropped into wine before drinking. It is said that the carbon on the bread reduced the acidity of the wine (which makes sense if you've ever tried any cheap Italian wine!).

Ten Toasts

10. Here's to the model husband, usually somebody else's.

9. Here's to every man here. May he be what he thinks himself to be.

8. Here is to the fools of the world...without them, the rest of us could not succeed.

7. May the most you wish for be the least you get!

6. While we live, let us live.

I have found my love! And if I go today I will have fulfilled my dreams. Finding a soul mate is one of the hardest things in life. If you believe in God he brings you the best things when you aren't looking. Don't be afraid and don't turn away. You might miss what he has brought you. Live for today. Learn from your past and pray and have hope for the future. Always remember, hope floats.
(Tray—30)

✗

I've been traveling the Sound now for 10 years. It has taken me from the home I've loved so dearly to the man my heart will be with for the rest of my life. The water has been both smooth and rough. To those who follow: Enjoy the ride whatever it may be, and remember always ride with the waves.
(Patti—49)

✗

I love Tonya.   (Jack—26)
✗
I love Jack.   (Tonya—26)

5. May you have the health of a salmon, a strong heart, and a wet mouth.

4. Here's health to the men, and may the ladies live forever.

3. Here's to prosperity...and the wisdom to use it well.

2. May you live as long as you like...and have all you like as long as you live.

My favorite toast:

1. May you be in heaven a half hour before the devil knows you're dead.

Beautiful is the person sitting next to me.
(Heather—30)

¤

The way a man treats the waitress on your third
date is how he will treat you in six months.
(Woman—32)

¤

I was away with my girl all weekend in romantic
Newport, but all I could think about was my dog,
Buddy. Should I still marry her? (Man—45)

¤

I am dating my best friend's girlfriend. Shh!
(Anon.)

¤

I'm the one dating him, and I'm eyeing his friend
Bill on this ferry. Shh, don't tell. (Anon.)

Layering Shooters Like a Pro

Layering is a technique that allows different liquors to float one on top of another in a glass, so they produce a pleasing aesthetic as well as an anesthetic effect. For layering technique, see page 128. This table will help you layer different alcohols. Each alcohol has its own weight, or specific gravity. These values tell you in what order that you should pour them. You must pour the heaviest liquors, or the liquors with the largest value, first. The lightest is 0.97, and the heaviest is 1.18.

Southern Comfort	0.97
Tuaca	0.98
Green Chartreuse	1.01
Cointreau	1.04
Peach liquor	1.04
Sloe gin	1.04
Peppermint Schnapps	1.04
Benedictine and brandy	1.04
Cherry liquor	1.04
Midori Melon liquor	1.05
Fruit flavored brandies	1.06

I met the nicest guy in my life on this boat. But unfortunately, I was with my peers from work and had dinner plans.   (Janet—46)

¤

I believed in Santa Claus, and he turned out to be my parents. Now I believe in the Devil, and I'm pretty sure it's my girlfriend. (John—22)

¤

There once was an old man of Lyme
Who married three wives at a time,
When asked "Why a third?"
He replied, "One's absurd!
And bigamy, Sir, is a crime!"
—William Cosmo Monkhouse

Campari	1.06
Yellow Chartreuse	1.06
Benedictine D.O.M.	1.07
Strawberry	1.08
Drambuie	1.08
Frangelico	1.08
Amaretto de Saranno	1.08
Tia Maria	1.09
Apricot liquor	1.09
Blackberry liquor	1.10
Blue Curacao	1.10
Galliano	1.11
Crème de Menthe	1.12
Coffee liquor	1.13
Crème de Banana	1.14
Crème de Cacao	1.14
Kahlua	1.14
Crème de Almond	1.16
Crème de Noyaux	1.16
Anisette	1.18
Grenadine	1.18
Crème de Cassis	1.18

Be careful of the toes you step on today because they may be connected to the legs that are connected to the ass you'll have to kiss tomorrow. (Valerie—44) P.S. I'm married to the man from Nantucket!

¤

I AM the man from Nantucket! (Man—44)

¤

To all women!!! When it comes to men, FOLLOW YOUR GUT, it will never steer your wrong. (Christine—29)

¤

Interesting—the people I meet, they all seem to be drawn to me; especially the strange ones. Actually, mostly the strange ones. (Karen—31)

Oh, No—Not Here Too!

Well, I don't think you want to know this, but here is a list of how much of that good sip is going to your hips.

Category	Alcohol Volume (%)	Calories per ounce
Wine, red or white	12	23
Champagne	12.5	26
American beer, non-micro	4.5	12
Liqueurs	12–24	86–105
Liquor, 80 proof	40	65
Liquor, 86 proof	43	70
Liquor, 90 proof	45	74

These stats don't include the mixers!

If a man says something in the forest and there is no woman around to hear him, is he still wrong? (Man—42)

ᴕ

Bob says, "I thought all men were created equal until I went into the locker room!" (Man—22)

ᴕ

I sit here at one end of the bar watching a 40-something couple kissing at the other end of the bar—oblivious to the crowd around them, and I have two thoughts:
Take it elsewhere.
How lucky for them.
(Woman—41)

ᴕ

People who get paid for sex are obviously better looking than the people who pay for sex. (Pete—21)

Island Breeze
1½ oz. light rum
4 oz. pineapple juice
1 oz. cranberry juice
2 dashes Angostura bitters
Lime wedge

Combine all ingredients (except lime) over ice in highball glass. Garnish with lime wedge.

Malibu Bay Breeze
1½ oz. Malibu rum
4 oz. pineapple juice
1½ oz. cranberry juice
Lime wedge

Build ingredients in highball glass and garnish with lime.

God gave men both a penis and a brain, but unfortunately not enough blood supply to run both at the same time. (Anon.)

¤

Don't kiss sleeping passengers on any ferry. (Woman—24)

¤

Don't sweat the petty stuff, just pet the sweaty stuff. (Colleen—31)

¤

I'm such a good lover because I practice a lot on my own. (Man—40)

¤

If you think sex is a pain in the ass, you're doing it backwards. (Man—41)

Word Origins

In 19th century America, *cock* was another word for "tap," and the last muddy dregs of the tap was its *tail.* Colonel Carter, of Culpepper Court House, Virginia, was served this insult at his local tavern. He threw it on the floor and shouted, "Hereafter I will drink cocktails of my own brewing!" His concoction, a mix of gin, lemon peel, bitters, and sugar, is the grandfather of the modern cocktail.

There are only two colors in wine: red and white. Any wine containing the slightest tinge of red is a red wine.

In the wine trade, the word *dry* means "lacking in sugar."

Sex is like air. It's not important unless you aren't getting any. (Man—22)

¤

Marriage: Anyone who thinks marriage is a fifty-fifty proposition doesn't understand women, or fractions. —Danny Thomas

¤

Don't worry, it only seems kinky the first time. (Man—32)

¤

What do electric trains and breasts have in common? They're intended for children, but men usually play with them. (Woman—41)

¤

Sex is like pizza, when it's good, it's very good, and when it's bad it's still pretty good. (Larry—30)

Wines with less than 14 percent alcohol will improve after bottling.

France consumes and produces more wine per capita than any other nation.

There are approximately 49 million bubbles in a bottle of champagne, according to scientist Bill Lembeck. Bill, get a life.

It takes approximately 600 grapes to produce a bottle of wine.

At the age of 52, Robert Mondavi started the Mondavi Winery in Napa Valley, California.

A good marriage depends on two things: finding the right person and being the right person. (Bill—32)

❈

If marriage were outlawed, only outlaws would have in-laws. (Woman—42)

❈

By all means marry. If you get a good wife, you will be happy, and if you get a bad one, you will become a philosopher.   —Socrates (Man—52)

❈

A happy wife is a happy life.
(Just married man—39)

❈

Trust your husband, adore your husband, and get as much as you can in your own name. (Woman—68)

Burden of *Proof*

Before the making of distilled spirits became skilled, primitive brewers had a very simple method for determining the drinkable strength of the spirit. An equal amount of spirit and gunpowder were mixed and a flame applied. If the gunpowder failed to burn, the spirit was too weak; if it burned too brightly, the spirit was too strong. But if the mixture burned evenly, with a blue flame, it was said to have been "proved." From this, we have adopted the term *proof*.

Always have at least one pound of ice cubes on hand per person per hour. For outside parties in warm weather, you will need more.

Keep your mixers refrigerated. You will save ice and make better drinks.

I just got married today to the most wonderful man in my life. I guess it's right what they say "Dreams really do come true." (Albertine—32)

¤

My definition of marriage—it resembles a pair of shears, so joined that they cannot be separated, often moving in opposite directions, yet always punishing anyone who comes between them.
—Sydney Smith (Sy—35)

¤

Key to a happy marriage: Never go to bed mad. Stay up and fight. —Phyllis Diller (Ward—65)

¤

Women marry men hoping they will change. Men marry women hoping they will not change. But I still love all the women. (Artie—50)

Don't shake cocktails containing carbonated mixers. You could get wet, and it makes the drink flat.

People get intoxicated faster when sitting down rather than when standing or walking.

The highest price ever paid for distilled spirits at auction was $79,552 for a 50-year-old bottle of Glenfiddich whiskey in the 1990s.

It is illegal to drink alcohol in Saskatchewan, Canada, while watching exotic dancers.

It was against the law to serve alcohol to a gay person in California in the 1940s.

In Uruguay, intoxication is a legal excuse for having an accident while driving.

To My Loving Husband: We've been married for almost 33 years. We went through the 60s together, watched men walk on the moon, went to Woodstock together, gave birth to two wonderful kids who grew up into wonderful adults that we are proud to know. We raised our family on Long Island, and we flourished. Now we're heading back on the ferry tonight after visiting our kids, who we see at least once a month in Massachusetts. I played with our grandson, Ben, all weekend while you worked on Lisa's house. Dan, our beautiful son, came to help, too.

How lucky we are to still be so very much in love, to be best friends, to have raised such a wonderful family. We have good jobs, good friends, a wonderful family. We are truly blessed.

No hateful foreigner who is jealous of our American lives can take away what we have.

I will always love you, and I know you will always love me. We always have each other unto eternity. (Your loving wife and the grandmother of your grandchildren, Linda—66)

The deep indentation on the bottom of a wine bottle is called a *punt*. It makes the bottle sturdier.

Idaho has the highest per person wine consumption rate in the United States.

White wines are best served chilled at 55–60 degrees Fahrenheit.

Red wines are best at 62–67 degrees Fahrenheit.

Most champagnes are made from red grapes.

Gin Rickey
$1\frac{1}{2}$ oz. gin
$\frac{1}{2}$ oz. fresh lime juice
5 oz. club soda
Lime wedge

Build gin, lime juice and club soda in a highball glass with ice. Garnish with lime.

If you want to be criticized, get married.
(Man—51)

✄

When a man steals your wife, there is no better revenge than to let him keep her. (Sacha—41)

✄

Key to my 43 year marriage: We have a perfect understanding. I'm perfect and she understands it.
(Ward—65)

✄

My wife is the best. (Man—40)

✄

It is better to copulate than never. —Robert Heinlein

There are 31 gallons of beer in a barrel. That's about 330 twelve-ounce beer cans, folks. A keg of beer has 15½ gallons.

Researchers at the U.S. Department of Agriculture say that laboratory rats that drink beer live six times longer than rats that drink just water.

Ten percent of the Russian government's income comes from the sales of vodka.

Americans spend approximately $25 billion each year on beer.

The vintage date on a bottle of wine indicates the year the grapes were picked, not the year of bottling.

To determine the percentage of alcohol in a bottle of liquor, divide the proof by two.

I don't know how it happened, maybe had something to do with 9/11, or maybe I just noticed her smile, but I started an affair with a married woman who worked for me. In my mind it is OK, but I am not sure, since I am married as well. I don't think my wife will ever know, but then again, my actions may give me away. I also fight with my feelings for Carrie (other woman). She is sexy, slender, funny, and has an amazing kiss. Her smell disorients me. The taste of her kiss intoxicates me. How long can I last to not fall in love, especially in times where life and people are so important? (Anon.)

¤

I don't know how it happened! Two people, two separate lives, so much to lose. Is it possible to love or be in love with two people? Is it wrong? How can it be, when it feels so good? The best way to say it is "Live each day as if it is your last." (Anon.)

When informed that General Ulysses S. Grant drank whiskey while leading his troops, President Abraham Lincoln, reportedly replied, "Find out the name of the brand so I can give it to my other generals."

Beer was not sold in bottles until 1850; it was not sold in cans until 1935.

A raisin dropped into a glass of champagne will repeatedly travel between the top and the bottom of the glass.

The shallow champagne glass originated with Marie Antoinette. Legend says that it was first formed from wax molds of her breasts.

You should never say anything to a woman that even remotely suggests that you think she's pregnant unless you can see an actual baby emerging from her at that moment. (Anon.)

¤

My wife and I thought we knew what love was, until we had a daughter.... Now we do. (Dave—35)

¤

The best thing you can do for your children is love your wife. (Bob—54)

¤

Having a baby is like trying to push a grand piano through a transom. —Alice Roosevelt Longworth

Jello Shooters

Empty one small packet of your favorite flavor Jell-O brand gelatin into a bowl. Pour in one cup of boiling water. Stir to dissolve. Let cool to room temperature. Add one cup of vodka. Pour into mold or pan. Freeze until firm. Cut into serving-size pieces.

The longest recorded champagne cork flight (straight up) was 177 feet and 9 inches, beginning four feet from level ground.

Foot treading of grapes is still used in producing a small quantity of the best port wines.

Vintage port can take 40 years to reach maturity.

Methyphobia is fear of alcohol.

The region of the United States that consumes the least alcohol (commonly known as the Bible Belt) is also known by many doctors as Stroke Alley.

We are returning from a Pee-Wee B hockey tournament in Massachusetts. We won! Great time, great fun, and we made the ferry.

¤

Kids keep you honest; company keeps your house clean. (Woman—46)

¤

Children need models more than they need critics. —Joseph Joubert (Man—52)

¤

Kids are your life—take care, love, and "take in the life." (Staci—33)

¤

Some time in your 20s you'll realize your father was usually right. (Bill—32)

In ancient Babylon, the bride's father would supply his son-in-law with all the mead (fermented honey beverage) he could drink for the first month after the wedding. Because their ancient calendar was lunar, or moon-based, this period of free mead was called the "honey month," what we now call the honeymoon.

Some scholars believe that the honeymoon originated in the old Norse custom of kidnapping a bride, and holding her in secret until the families could agree on terms for the wedding.

Andrew went to Quinnipiac University yesterday. Andrew was our last bird in the nest. Now he's out. We pray for him and those in his life whom he will influence.
(Francis, 51, and Nancy, 50)

¤

Cherish your parents. No matter what they have done, they did the best they could, and they will not be here with us forever. Take time out to enjoy the little things in life. (Tracy—31)

¤

Raising teenagers is like nailing Jell-O to a tree. (Anon.)

¤

Familiarity breeds contempt—and children.
—Mark Twain

Before thermometers were invented, brewers would dip a thumb or finger into the liquid to determine the ideal temperature, neither too hot nor too cold, for adding yeast. From this we get the phrase "rule of thumb."

In English pubs, drinks are served in pints and quarts. In old England, bartenders would advise unruly customers to mind their own pints and quarts. It's the origin of "Mind your Ps and Qs."

Rather than continue sailing, the Pilgrims landed at what is now Plymouth, Massachusetts, because they were running out of alcoholic beverages and other vital supplies.

The Manhattan cocktail (whiskey and sweet vermouth) was invented by Winston Churchill's mother, Jennie.

You can tell a child is growing up when he stops asking where he came from and starts refusing to tell you where he is going. (Man—52)

¤

Those who say "God doesn't give you more than you can handle" have never lived with a teenage girl! (Terry—34)

¤

Anne and Tom are on this boat because they are leaving their son in Mass. to start his own life. (Anon.)

¤

Life really starts after your kids grow up; and it ends when you start taking care of your parents. Hopefully the space between these two events is huge. (Woman—43)

Alcohol is considered the only proper payment for teachers among the Lepcha people of Tibet.

Ohio state law prohibits getting a fish drunk.

In the 1600s, thermometers were filled with brandy instead of mercury.

"I hadn't the heart to touch my breakfast. I told Jeeves to drink it himself."
　　　　　　　　—P.G. Wodehouse, *My Man Jeeves*

"Claret is the liquor for boys, port for men, but he who aspires to be a hero must drink brandy."
　　　　　　　　Dr. Samuel Johnson

A father's legacy is his children. Love and care for them well. (Joe—36)

¤

If I had known my grandson was going to be so good, I would have had my grandson before my daughter.   (Ed—41)

¤

We just passed the section of the Long Island Sound where my father was buried at sea a year ago. He was a great father, and I miss him greatly. (Anon.)

¤

I lost my dad today. I grieve, I ask why, and there are no responses or reasons given. Why, I ask, at the age of 52. Yes, 52. All I can say is I am always going to remember him. In my life, I'll love him more. (Sean—23)

Warming Up

The temperature at which a wine is served has an immense impact on its taste.

Wine Type	Fahrenheit	Centigrade
Sparkling wine	42–54	6–10
Rosé wine	48–54	9–12
White wine	48–58	9–14
Sherry (light)	48–58	9–14
Red wine	57–68	13–20
Fortified wine	57–68	13–20
Sherry (dark)	57–68	13–20

On the Wings of a Prayer...

I set you free on the wings of a prayer; to fly
through life in his tender care.

You're free from the nest and the ties that are
bound; free from the pressures I carry around

If I kept you I'd only be cutting your wings;
not offering the chance a true family brings.

The decision I've made has my heart torn in two;
but I know what I'm doing is the best thing for
you.

The sky is so vast, the mountains so high;
take wing and remember: I LOVE YOU. GOODBYE.

(Marylou—17, on the pain of placing a child up for
adoption)

Order Up

When building a drink, always put sugar, fruit juice, other ingredients in glass first. Add liquor last. When the recipe calls for carbonated soda, start with ice, liquor, etc. Mix the soda (cold) in last.

If you need to chill a bottle of wine in a hurry, 35 minutes in the freezer will do the trick.

The three steps in wine tasting: look, smell, and taste.

It's easy to have frosted glasses for your friends: Just put the glasses in the freezer or bury them long enough in ice cubes to create a white frosted look on the glass.

Don't treat your family and loved ones as if there will always be tomorrow to apologize or to hug them and tell them how much you really do love them. I thought this way, and I lost my father unexpectedly. Now I suffer. I love you, Papi. I'm sorry. (Elvis—30)

¤

Happiness is having a large, loving, caring, close-knit family in another city. (Man—61)

¤

"It wouldn't hurt us to be nice, would it?"
"That depends on your threshold of pain."
—George S. Kaufman, on being told his aunt was coming to visit

¤

Hug your loved ones today because you don't know where they'll be tomorrow. (Man—41)

Keep vodka in the freezer for best results.

It's a good idea to have enough liquor on hand to serve at least one drink per person per hour.

Most of the time, light beers move three times as fast as regular beer. So for your party, buy more light and serve ice cold.

There's nothing more important than family.
(Jerry—57)

¤

"To lose one parent, Mr. Worthing, may be regarded as a misfortune; to lose both looks like carelessness." —Oscar Wilde

¤

I just spent a weekend with my two younger brothers and my father, who is 74; that's when you realize how precious life is, and how important your memories are. It's a shame that my mom and my dad's best friend of 49 years were not there in body to enjoy it, but she was there in spirit and our love for her was as strong if not stronger for her. Enjoy life every second you breathe, because someday you won't be there to share the memories, you will be the memory... so make them great memories. Enjoy life. (Bruce—50)

So, You Want to Be a Barman?

Recipe for a Successful Barman
1 very large measure of infinite patience
1 jigger of humor
2 cups of good conversation about everything
(especially sports)
1 dash tolerance
1 sprinkle of psychic power (to see trouble coming
before it starts)
1 garnish (cheerful smile)
1 postgraduate degree in multitasking skills
(mixing, serving, counting money, stocking bar,
checking IDs, watching everybody and everything
in the bar, and talking, all at the same time.)

Mix all ingredients and serve straight up.

Why? Why do they call them ex's when they say, "*Why* did I marry her?" (Steve—41)

¤

Love is grand; divorce is a hundred grand. (Man—52)

¤

Never get married twice! (Doug—38)

¤

Do you know why divorce costs so much? Because it's worth it! (Lingerfelt—30)

¤

When a divorced man marries a divorced woman, four get into bed. —The Talmud

Holiday Drinks

The Christmas Shooter, or Santa Shot

½ oz. Grenadine
½ oz. Green Crème de Menthe
½ oz. Peppermint Schnapps

Layer ingredients in a shot glass.
Tastes like a candy cane.

Hot Rummed Cider

1½ qt. apple cider
6 tbsp. sugar
3 tbsps. butter
1½ cups light rum

Bring cider and sugar to a boil in large saucepan.
Reduce heat and add butter. When butter is
melted, add rum. Serve in a heatproof punch bowl
or pitcher. Serves 6–8.

I know this has to be true: As we walk through life, many of us will want to blame our failures on our parents and what they haven't done *for* us or what they have done *to* us. Let go of all excuses, no matter how long you have been going down the wrong road. It is never too late to turn around. Be great, achieve all that you can, and perhaps instead of blaming our failures on others, we can simply keep our accomplishments within and not give credit where it may not be due. Live for yourself and let go of your parents' suppression. (Jon—21)

¤

Life is about the passing of time, about the stealthy merging of youth into age, the invisibility of the traps in our own characters, into which we walk unwary, unknowing.
Max Beerbohm (Leslie-66)

Winter Cider
1 gal. apple cider
6 cinnamon sticks
1½ cups rum
1 cup peach brandy
¼ cup peach schnapps
Cinnamon sticks for garnish
Apple slices

In large saucepan, bring cider and cinnamon to a full boil over medium heat. Reduce heat and add rum, brandy, and schnapps, stirring until heated through. Serve in Irish coffee glasses, garnished with a cinnamon stick and an apple slice.
Serves 18-20.

Ex-wives are what you make them. (Wife #2—42)

✕

Getting divorced just because you don't love a man is almost as silly as getting married because you do. —Zsa Zsa Gabor

✕

To everyone that has problems: Hang out with people who are smarter than you, and buy them coffee. (Man—26)

✕

The Red Sox WILL win a World Series in my lifetime! (David—43)

Holiday Punch

Hot Burgundy Punch
¼ cup sugar
1½ cups boiling water
Peel of ½ lemon
1 three-inch cinnamon stick
5 whole cloves
½ tsp. ground allspice
1 cup apple juice
1 750-ml. bottle burgundy wine
½ tsp. nutmeg

In large saucepan, dissolve sugar in boiling water. Add lemon peel, cinnamon, cloves, allspice, and apple juice. Cook over moderately high heat for 15 minutes.

Strain into another saucepan and add wine. Simmer over low heat, but do not boil. Serve hot in heat-proof cups with a sprinkle of nutmeg. Serves 16.

Life is a wonderful thing if you experience it to the fullest. There can be great joy, happiness, and fulfillment, yet life cannot be complete unless you have experienced the other side, that of loss, sadness and tragedy. With that we can feel the entirety of life, beginning and end. Your life begins to have more meaning and purpose, more strength from within, more emotion and compassion for others. It's a strange thing, but if you learn from all that is dealt you throughout the years you can become someone who will give strength to others who may not have gone through the "experiences" yet. Enjoy your life through all the positive as well as the negative, and smile – it will give joy to others. Life is a wonderful thing.
(Woman—48)

¤

'Poe,' I said, 'was perhaps the first great nonstop literary drinker of the American nineteenth century. He made the indulgences of Coleridge and De Quincey seem like a bit of mischief in the kitchen with the cooking sherry.'
James Thurber,
Alarms and Diversions

A Drink for Every Letter in the Alphabet

Amaretto and Cream

1 oz. Amaretto
1½ oz. cream

Stir in an old-fashioned glass over ice.

Brave Bull

1 oz. Kahlua
1 oz. tequila

Pour over ice in an old-fashioned glass.

Chapala

¾ oz. lemon juice
dash grenadine
dash Triple Sec
1½-2 oz. orange juice

Stir all ingredients over crushed ice in Collins glass.

Fall seven times. Get up eight. (Carole—53)

¤

No longer give strength to that from which you wish to be free. (Molly—44)

¤

Hard times get easier when you keep your chin up and a smile on your face. (Heather—21)

¤

Find a job you love and you will never work a day of your life. —Confucius (Man—52)

¤

Come forth, Lazarus! And he came fifth and lost the job. —James Joyce, *Ulysses*

Dirty Mother

1½ oz. brandy
1 oz. Kahlua

Serve over ice in a rocks glass.

El Presidente Cocktail #1

Juice of 1 lime
1 tsp. Pineapple Juice
1 tsp. Grenadine
1½ oz. light rum

Shake all ingredients with ice and strain into cocktail glass.

It's great to quit a job you hate. (Man—45)

¤

The human race is faced with a cruel choice: work or daytime television. (Anon.)

¤

This is what I know to be true: The less time I have to work, the more things I get done. (Man—82)

¤

I have long been of the opinion that if work were such a splendid thing the rich would have kept more of it for themselves.   —Bruce Grocott

¤

Don't fear retirement—you will be so busy, you won't know how you had the time to work. (Tom—72)

Freddie Fudpucker

1½ oz. tequila
5 oz. orange juice
Float of Galliano

Build tequila and orange juice in a highball glass over ice. Top with Galliano.
Note: lemon juice = sour mix.

Golden Nail

1½ oz. bourbon
¾ oz. Southern Comfort

Stir ingredients over ice cubes in small highball glass.

Borrow money from pessimists—they don't expect it back. (Anon.)

¤

Give a man all the money he would ever want, and only then you will truly know him. (Tony—58)

¤

Why is there so much month left at the end of the money? —Maurice Chevalier/John Barrymore

¤

Never invest your money in anything that eats or needs repair. (Man—42)

¤

Cocaine is God's way of saying you're making too much money. (Man—44)

Harvey Wallbanger

1 oz. vodka
4 oz. orange juice
½ oz. Galliano

Pour vodka and orange juice into Collins glass over
ice cubes. Stir. Float Galliano on top.

Irish Coffee

1½ oz. Irish whiskey
brown sugar
1 cup strong hot coffee
Whipped cream

Heat whiskey in a heat-resistant glass (do not
boil). Add sugar. Fill with hot coffee, stir, top with
cream.

Funny how a $10 bill looks so big at church and so small at the mall...or the bar.   (Woman—56)

¤

Love people and use money... not the other way around. (Woman—43)

¤

Money does not make unhappy people happy, and happy people don't need money. (Anon.)

¤

His money is twice tainted: 'Tain't yours and 'tain't mine.   —Mark Twain

John Collins

1½ oz. bourbon
4 oz. sour mix
Lemon-lime soda
Orange

Blend bourbon and sour mix. Top with lemon-lime soda. Garnish with orange.

Kamikaze

1 oz. sour mix
1 oz. Triple Sec
1 oz. vodka

Shake all ingredients and serve over ice in an Old-Fashioned glass.

A fool and her money are soon courted.
—Helen Rowland

¤

Money couldn't buy friends, but you get a better
class of enemy. (Man—41)

¤

A bank is a place that will lend you money if you can
prove that you don't need it. —Bob Hope

¤

Live, love, and be happy – life is shorter than you
think! In the scheme of life, we are a single grain
of sand on the beach. Live every day as if it were
your last – because it may be your last! SAVOR
EVERY DAY! (Elaine—53, two-time cancer
survivor)

Lynchburg Lemonade

1 ½ oz. Jack Daniel's
1 oz. Triple Sec or Cointreau
7-Up
Lemon wedge
Orange slice

Shake the first three ingredients with ice and strain into an ice-filled highball glass. Top with 7-Up and garnish with the lemon wedge and orange slice.

Melon Ball

1 oz. Midori melon liqueur
1 oz. vodka
2 oz. pineapple juice

Pour all ingredients over ice in a highball glass and garnish with an orange, pineapple, or watermelon slice.

Failure has no friends. —John F. Kennedy

¤

Life is not a rehearsal, so when you get the chance, go for it. (Holly—40)

¤

Regrets: not many. Call me a dreamer—but if I don't dream before I die, I will look back with regret and feel sad that I never dreamed and never tried. Follow your dreams. It's *your* life. (Man—31)

¤

A little loneliness is a small price to pay for freedom. (Mouse—67)

Nutty Irishman

1 oz. Bailey's Irish Cream
1 oz. Frangelico

Shake and strain ingredients over ice in a rocks glass.

Orgasm

¾ oz. Irish Cream
¾ oz. coffee liqueur
2 oz. Half & Half

Pour ingredients over ice. Strain into another glass.

Peppermint Stick

1 oz. peppermint Schnapps
1½ oz. Crème de Cacao (white)
1 oz. light cream

Shake ingredients with ice and strain into champagne flute.

If *A* is a success in life, then *A* equals *x* plus *y* plus *z*. Work is *x*, *y* is play; and *z* is keeping your mouth shut. —Albert Einstein

¤

After you are dead and buried, no one will care what size your house was or what kind of import you drove. They will remember *you*. So be kind to others and enjoy life. Live! (Lisa—39)

¤

Twenty years from now you will be more disappointed by the things you didn't do than by the ones you did. So throw off the bowlines, sail away from the safe harbor. Catch the trade winds in your sails. Explore. Dream. (Man—53)

¤

If you have to hold onto something, then you've already lost it. (Ed—34)

Quaalude

1 oz. vodka
1 oz. hazelnut liqueur
1 oz. coffee liqueur
1 splash milk

Pour all ingredients over ice in Old-Fashioned glass.

Robin's Nest

1 oz. vodka
1 oz. cranberry juice
½ oz. Crème de Cacao (white)

Shake with ice and strain into cocktail glass.

Sidecar

1 oz. sour mix
½ oz. Triple Sec
1 oz. brandy

Shake with ice and strain into cocktail glass.

The richness of a man is not measured by how much he has, but by how little he needs. (Man—39)

✄

If you're comfortable in life, you're going nowhere. (Jeff—25)

✄

Fears over tomorrow and regrets over yesterday are twin thieves that rob us of the moment. (Man—52)

✄

The optimist proclaims that we live in the best of all possible worlds, and the pessimist fears this is true. —James Branch Cabell

Toasted Almond

1½ oz. coffee liqueur
1 oz. Amaretto
1½ oz. cream or milk

Combine all ingredients over ice in an Old-Fashioned glass.

Ultimate June Bug

1 oz. Midori melon liqueur
2¾ oz. Malibu rum
1 oz. sour mix
1 oz. pineapple juice

Blend all ingredients over ice in a Collins glass.

Don't be afraid to change a recipe slightly to suit your tastes!

I was the leader of the Cannonball Run, 2001. When the cop stopped me doing 74 m.p.h. on the way to catch this ferry, he said I was such a good guy he let me go. (Tom—53)

ꭓ

I'm the cop that stopped Tom during the Cannonball Run. We just wanted him out of our state. (Anon.)

ꭓ

Don't be sorry... be careful; you will be a lot less sorry that way. (Woman—23)

ꭓ

If you face what you're afraid of, you find out what you're made of. (Man—36)

ꭓ

Live life on the edge—less crowded, better view! (Frank—41)

Vodka Stinger

1 oz. vodka
1 oz. Crème de Menthe (white)
Shake ingredients with ice and strain into cocktail glass.

Watermelon

Vodka
Strawberry liqueur
Sweet and sour mix
Orange juice

Serve equal parts over ice in a Collins glass.

X, y, z

1 tsp. lemon juice
$\frac{1}{2}$ oz. Triple Sec
1 oz. light rum

Shake all ingredients with ice and strain into cocktail glass.

Live life to the max... enjoy yourself and don't hold back because you'll miss out on something you'll regret either tomorrow or years from now.
(Jennifer—21)

¤

It's a good day if I'm a little better than I was yesterday. (Brian—44)

¤

GOTTA LIVE! (Anon.)

Yellow Bird

2 oz. rum
½ oz Triple Sec
½ oz. Galliano
¾ oz. fresh lime juice
Lime, for garnish

Shake all the ingredients with ice and strain into a chilled cocktail or martini glass. Garnish with lime peel.

Zaza Cocktail

1½ oz. gin
¾ oz. Dubonnet
Orange peel

Stir ingredients with ice into cocktail glass. Add a twist of orange peel.

I had a good day today. (Anon.)

¤

Judge your success by what you had to give up in order to get it. (Man—48)

¤

Success is not measured by the amount of money you have, it's measured by the love you have and share. (Anon.)

¤

I don't know the secret of success...
But I know the secret of failure...
trying to please everyone. (Sean—31)

¤

Success is getting what you want, and happiness is wanting what you get. — (Dave)

For a dinner party, plan on about two glasses of wine per person.

Young wines should be served cooler than older wines, and it is always better to serve a wine too cold than too warm.

If you are on a budget or lack space to store both red and white wine glasses, buy all-purpose 10-ounce wine glasses and use them for both red and white wines.

Never use wine for cooking that you do not consider fit to drink.

Want salt on your margarita glass? Before preparing the drink, wipe the rim of the glass with a slice of lime and dip it in coarse salt.

One man's success is another man's folly, is another's love, is another's envy, is another's passion, is another's jealousy. In other words, it is all relative, so if it makes you happy, it is truly success... if it does not, then is it really success? (Charles—34)

¤

It takes twenty years to make an overnight success. —Attributed to Eddie Cantor

¤

In the race to be better or best, do not miss the joy of being. (Melissa—23)

¤

I thank God I live in a country where dreams can come true, where failure sometimes is the first step to success, and where success is only another form of failure if we forget what our priorities should be. (Woman—44)

Cream Dreams

After Five
1 oz. Irish Cream
1 oz. Peppermint Schnapps
$\frac{1}{2}$ oz. Kahlua

Shake with ice and strain into cocktail glass.

Chocolate Cherry
$\frac{1}{2}$ oz. Kahlua
$\frac{1}{2}$ oz. Grenadine
$\frac{1}{2}$ oz. Irish Cream

Layer Grenadine, Kahlua, and then Irish Cream.

One day you realize you are whatever it is you were going to be. (Charlie—62)

¤

Only the sinner has a right to preach. (Woman—59)

¤

Whether you believe or not... there *is* someone watching over you. (June—46)

¤

Jesus is coming—everyone look busy. (Man—48)

¤

Jesus loves you! You have every reason to be happy. (Julia—17)

Cream Coconut Frappe
2 parts Irish Cream
1 part Malibu rum
2 parts milk

Shake with ice and strain into cocktail glass.

Cream Dream
2 oz. Bailey's Irish Cream
2 oz. Half & Half

Pour cold Irish Cream into champagne flute and slowly float the Half & Half on top.

Irish Dublin Double
1 part Irish Cream
1 part Amaretto – shot

Shake with ice and strain into cordial glass.

Your talent is God's gift to you, what you do with it is your gift to him. (Bob—38)

✠

All sentences that start with "God forbid" describe what is possible. —Jewish saying

✠

God gave us lots of gifts, and if there is one that I know of, it is true acceptance. Accept people for who they are and treat them accordingly!!
P.S. And remember bartenders are *gods*—don't piss off the gods! (Johnny—34)

✠

Thank you Lord for bestowing on me health, happiness and a wonderful soul mate!
(Mary Ann—50)

Brandy can only be labeled as cognac only if it is produced in the designated growing areas in the Charentes region of France.

Toast: May you live as long as you want, and never want as long as you live.

When a bartender gives you your drink and then knocks on the bar, it's a free drink. Lucky you!

VSOP means Very Special Old Pale.

Good idea, this book. I just visited my newly widowed cousin and his family on Long Island. Only life and each other matter, as does the importance of facing God on judgment day and being able to tell him, "I did my best my entire life to follow the path of your son." (Woman—42)

¤

Never give and then hang around waiting for the favor to be returned. Be excellent to one another even when there's nothing in it for you.
(Leonard—28)

¤

Everyone should believe in something. I believe I'll have another drink. — W.C.Fields

¤

Religions change; beer and wine remain.
—Hervey Allen

How Much Is in Your Bottle?

Name	Capacity	Bottles
Bottle	.75	1
Magnum	1.50	2
Jeroboam	3.00	4
Rehoboam	4.50	6
Methuselah	6.00	8
Salmanazar	9.00	12
Balthazar	12.00	16
Nebuchadnezzar	15.00	20

He was a wise man who invented God. —Plato

¤

Plato was a bore.—Nietzsche

¤

It doesn't cost anything to be kind. Love brings you together; friends and trust keep you together. (Barbara, 30, and Bernie, 33)

¤

Treat every person with kindness and respect, even those who are rude to you. Remember that you show compassion to others not because of who they are but because of who you are. (Kathy—34)

Layering

To pour liqueurs into a glass, simply use the rounded, or back, part of a spoon and rest it against the inside of the glass. Slowly pour down onto the spoon. The liqueur should run down the inside of the glass and smoothly layer. This technique takes practice but can be mastered by anyone. Remember - add the heaviest liqueurs first. See the chart on pages 52 & 54.

Note: if you mess up the layers, place the shooter in the refrigerator for about an hour and the liqueurs will separate themselves.

Cowboy

2 parts Butterscotch Schnapps
1 part Irish Cream

Fill a shot glass two-thirds with butterscotch Schnapps. Then carefully layer the Irish Cream on top to fill the glass.

I don't care what is written about me so long as it isn't true. —Dorothy Parker

¤

Be kind to yourself and it will rub off on all and forgive! (Frances—37)

¤

Beginning today, treat everyone you meet as if he or she were going to be dead by midnight. Extend to them all the care, kindness, and understanding you can muster, and do so with no thought of any reward. Your life will never be the same again. (Al—67)

¤

I saw an old man smile and wave at a little girl today, and it made everyone that saw it feel good.... It don't take much. (Anon.)

Bob's Old-Fashioned Favorite

There is no question that the Old-Fashioned is one of the oldest and best cocktails. It's also the drink I enjoy making the most when I am working.

1 teaspoon sugar
Slice of orange
1 cherry (Maraschino)
Squirt of soda or water
Dash Angostura bitters
2–3 oz. bourbon

Muddle sugar, orange, and cherry with the soda or water. Add a dash of bitters in the bottom of old-fashioned glass. Add bourbon and ice cubes.

Following the same recipe, you can also make an Old Fashioned with scotch or rye.

People can grow in many aspects of life. They can be successful in love, in sports, in their professions, with their families, with their friends and then what? Life's successes must be shared. If the trials and tribulations of one's life are not shared, how can younger generations learn more quickly and gain knowledge that has showed one's own generation to prosper? Teach others what is important; speak of the value of compassion, the strength of love, and the rewards of hard work. Share your knowledge and share your love— everyone will be better for it. (Man - 48)

¤

The truth will set you free. If it won't, better get a real good lawyer! (Phil—39)

¤

A truth that's told with bad intent beats all the lies you can invent. (Anon.)

Toasts Around the World

Language	Toast
Austrian	Prost / Zum Wohl
Brazilian	Saude
Chinese	Kong chien
Dutch	Proost
Egyptian	Fee sihetak
French	A votre sante / Sante
German	Prost
Greek	Gia'sou
Icelandic	Santanka nu / Skal
Indian	Apki Lambi Umar Ke Liye
Italian	Salute / Cin cin
Japanese	Kanpai
Korean	Konbe
Latin	Sanitas bona / Bene tibi
Mexican	Salud
Norwegian	Skal
Polish	Na zdrowie
Russian	Vashe zdorovie
Thai	Chook-die / Sawasdi
Turkish	Serefe
Yiddish	Le'chaim
Zulu	Oogy wawa

Always tell the truth. That way, you don't have to remember what you said. —Mark Twain (Woman—60)

¤

A half-truth is a whole lie. —Jewish saying

¤

When liars speak the truth, they are not believed. (Man—52)

¤

A happy person is an honest person. Telling the truth cleanses the soul. Be honest and be free! (Woman—46)

¤

Never lie; reason being it's just a temporary solution to a permanent problem that always comes back. (Bob—38)

Who's Counting?
There are 1.2 carbohydrates in 1 ounce of wine.

Two million cases of Jose Cuervo were sold in 1996.

There are 27 herbs and spices in Benedictine.

One bottle of The MaCallan 60-year-old sold for $30,000 in Glasgow, Scotland in April 2002.

Green Comfort
$\frac{1}{4}$ oz. vodka
$\frac{3}{4}$ oz. melon liqueur
$\frac{1}{4}$ oz. peach Schnapps
$\frac{1}{4}$ oz. Sprite or 7-Up
$\frac{1}{4}$ oz. pineapple juice

Mix all ingredients in shaker with ice and strain into shot glass.

Honesty is almost always the best policy.
(Mark—39)

¤

The eyes don't lie! (Woman—37)

¤

Paint makes it what it ain't. (George—29)

¤

Women are only really themselves before the age
of five and after the age of 50. (Man—55)

¤

The young know everything, middle aged suspect
everything, the old believe everything. (Oscar
Wilde)

Servings per person

Estimate by judging what you're serving... and if you are having any of *my* friends over, this gauge may be off just a tad.

Lunch

People	4	8	12	30	100
Cocktails	6	12	18	45	150
Glasses Of Wine	8	12	36	60	200
Liqueurs	4	8	12	30	100

Dinner Party

People	4	8	12	30	100
Cocktails	8	16	24	60	200
Glasses of Wine	8	16	24	60	200
Liqueurs	4	8	12	30	100

From birth to 18, a girl needs good parents. From 18 to 35, she needs good looks. From 35 to 55, good personality. From 55 on, she needs money.
—Sophie Tucker

¤

It's what you learn after you know it all that counts. (Bob—52)

¤

You teach best what you most need to learn. (Bob—38)

¤

Experience is a hard teacher. It gives the test before it presents the lesson. (Jim—39)

Evening Cocktails

People	4	8	12	30	100
Cocktails	16	24	48	120	400
Glasses of Wine	16	24	48	120	400

Note: Use in combination or singularly. Estimate by judging what you are serving and to whom you are serving.

Cosmopolitan
1¼ oz. vodka
½ oz. lime juice
¼ oz. Triple Sec or Cointreau
¼ oz. cranberry juice
Lime wedge

Shake all the ingredients well with ice and strain into martini glass. Garnish with lime wedge.

Learn from yesterday, live for today, hope for tomorrow. (Patty—41)

¤

Experience is the comb that nature gives us when we are bald. —Russian proverb

¤

Education and intelligence aren't the same thing! (Man—42)

¤

Sometimes it is better to know all the questions than all of the answers. (Heather—30)

¤

Better to be right slow than wrong fast. (Bill—43)

Salty Dog

Lime wedge
Salt and sugar, mixed, to coat rim of glass
2 oz. vodka
4 oz. grapefruit juice

Moisten the rim of an old-fashioned glass with lime wedge, and then roll the rim in a mixture of equal parts salt and sugar. Fill glass with ice cubes, add vodka and grapefruit juice. Stir.

Fifteen men on the dead man's chest
Yo-ho-ho and a bottle of rum!
Drink and the devil had done for the rest—
Yo-ho-ho and a bottle of rum!

—Robert Louis Stevenson,
Treasure Island

First with the head, then with the heart. (Matt—
28)

x

Wisdom comes with age, but sometimes age comes
alone. (Woman—21)

x

A lot of good arguments are spoiled by some fool
who knows what he's talking about. (Man—52)

x

Maturity is a high price to pay for growing up.
—Tom Stoppard

x

To be old and wise you must first be young and
stupid. (Man—21)

Chill Out with Warm Winter Drinks

Coffees

Coffee Royale
1½ oz. brandy
4 oz. coffee
1–2 tsps. sugar, or to taste
Whipped cream
Chocolate sprinkles

Pour brandy into clear coffee mug and fill with hot coffee. Add sugar and stir. Top with whipped cream. Serve with chocolate sprinkles.

Caribbean Coffee
1½ oz. dark rum
4 oz. coffee
1–2 tsps. sugar, or to taste
Heavy cream

Pour rum into clear coffee mug. Fill with coffee. Add sugar and stir. Add heavy cream.

The art of being wise is knowing what to overlook. (Woman—42)

¤

Self-knowledge is always bad news. (David—62)

¤

If ignorance is bliss, why aren't there more happy people?" (Sandra—48)

¤

A wise man will still always listen when one is talking. You can always tell when someone "knows it all." They are the first ones to interrupt and give their input. (Vic—37)

¤

To understand all is to forgive all. (Tommy—52)

Italian Coffee
1½ oz. Sambuca
4 oz. coffee
½ oz. heavy cream
Whipped cream

Pour Sambuca in clear coffee mug. Add coffee.
Stir in heavy cream. Top with whipped cream.

Hot Cocoa
Big Bob's Almond Joy
I introduced this drink to the ferry company, and
they named it after me.

1½ oz. Malibu rum
4 oz. hot cocoa
Whipped cream

Pour rum in coffee mug. Stir in cocoa. Top with
whipped cream.

Those who seek wisdom from random jottings of ferry boat passengers deserve their fate. (Bullet—42)

¤

Sometimes the road less traveled is less traveled for a reason! (Jerry—28)

¤

Do not speak unless what you have to say is more important than the silence that surrounds us. (William—23)

¤

If you keep your mouth shut you will never put your foot in it. —Austin O'Malley

¤

Sometimes you gotta do what you don't wanna do, to get to where you wanna be. (Bob—38)

Trivia from Behind the Bar...
Wines with less than 14 percent alcohol will improve after bottling.

Beer glasses should never be washed with soap or soapy water. The soap leaves a fatty film which breaks down the bubbles of the CO_2.

Lemons and oranges will give more juice if you first soak them in warm water. You can also place them in a microwave for ten seconds.

Mist: Any spirit served over crushed ice.

Spirits do not improve in glass. Once bottled, they remain unchanged.

France consumes and produces more wine than any other nation.

The only cure for a hangover is rest and time. Hiccups, however, are another story. See page 32.

You can't hold on to the past and ride off into the future. (Bob—38)

✗

Endure the unendurable; bear the unbearable; accept the unacceptable. (Kristen—31)

✗

When a man is angry, he cannot be in the right. (Anon.)

✗

I have often regretted my speech, never my silence. (Man—52)

✗

Nothing is opened more often by mistake than the mouth. (Woman—61)

Composition of Beer

Beer is one of the most complex of food products. Here is a percentage breakdown of beer's ingredients by weight:
Water: 89-90
Alcohol: 3.5–4 .0Carbohydrates: 4-5
Protein: 0.20–0.45
Carbon dioxide: 0.40–0.45
Mineral salts: 0.02

As you can see, the largest part of beer is water. From the point of view of health, beer is one of the finest beverages one can consume. The alcohol, with its food value, furnishes energy. The carbohydrates give strength. The proteins help us to assimilate food. The carbon dioxide (gas), which gives beer its head, helps to create the cooling or refreshing effect that makes beer so popular in the summertime. The hops bitters help stimulate the appetite.

The ideal temperature at which to serve beer is 45 degrees Fahrenheit.

Snowflakes individually are useless—but look what happens when they come together. (Jeannine—24)

¤

Closed minds should come with closed mouths. (Deborah—23)

¤

When I asked a high school English teacher how long the essay had to be, he replied, "It should be like a woman's skirt. Long enough to cover the subject, but short enough to keep it interesting!" (Greg—24)

¤

Life not only begins at 40, it begins to show. (Anon.)

¤

The older I get, the faster I was. (Kathy—40)

Classics

Here is a list of drinks I've made quite a few of in my years. America's favorites, they will always be around.

Bourbon (or Scotch) and Water

2 oz. bourbon or Scotch
4 oz. water

Pour bourbon or Scotch and water into an old-fashioned glass. Add ice and a twist of lemon if desired. Stir.

Bourbon, Scotch, or Vodka on the Rocks

2 oz. bourbon, Scotch, or vodka

Pour liquor into an old-fashioned glass half-filled with ice.

Wrinkles don't hurt. (Anon.)

¤

Middle age is when you choose your cereal for the fiber, not the toy. (Anon.)

¤

The most delightful advantage of being bald...one can hear snowflakes. (Man—61)

¤

I am 80 years old. But I don't know what I will do when I grow up. (Anon.)

¤

It's very true—to enjoy your life after 85, or older— because you haven't too many days left. Thank you, Bob. (Bill—85)

Backyard Bartender

Mixed drinks are an excellent alternative to barbecue punches at your summertime outdoor affairs. Here are some popular warm weather favorites:

Fourth of July Tooter

1 oz. grenadine
1 oz. vodka
1 oz. Blue Curacao

In cordial or shot glass, pour carefully, in order above, so that each ingredient floats on preceding one.

Margarita

Lemon or lime rind
Coarse salt
$1\frac{1}{2}$ oz. tequila
$\frac{1}{2}$ oz. Triple Sec
1 oz. lemon or lime juice

Rub rim of cocktail glass with rind of lemon or lime. Dip rim in salt. Shake remaining ingredients with ice and strain into salt-rimmed glass.

Remember, we're here for a good time, not a long time! (Robin—37)

☒

It is the malady of our age that the young are so busy teaching us that they have no time left to learn. —Eric Hoffer

☒

You don't stop laughing when you get old. You get old because you stop laughing. (Heather—21)

☒

Without memories, each day is the first, and each kiss is like the first. (Vincent—35)

☒

The game of life is going to end eventually for all of us. (Man—39)

Frozen Drinks
Don't forget the paper umbrellas!

Piña Colada
3 oz. light rum
2 oz. Coco Lopez
1 oz. heavy cream
1 cup crushed ice

Pour all the ingredients into a blender and blend for 20 seconds. Pour into Collins glass and garnish with pineapple wedge and cherry.

Banana Daiquiri
$1\frac{1}{2}$ oz. light rum
$\frac{3}{4}$ oz. fresh lime juice
1 tsp. sugar
1 tbsp. Triple Sec
1 medium banana, sliced

Blend the ingredients—reserving one slice of banana—with 1 cup of the crushed ice until smooth. Pour into champagne flute. Garnish with slice of banana.

Life is a path you create with your actions. (Anon.)

¤

If a man hasn't found anything worth dying for, it isn't worth living. (Matt—23)

¤

Living up to ideals is like doing everyday work with your Sunday clothes on. (Ed—28)

¤

Life is about living; living is about learning; learning is about loving. (Bob—38)

¤

The little things? The little moments? They aren't little. (Bob—52)

Strawberry Daiquiri
1½ oz. light rum
½ oz. Maraschino liqueur
4–6 medium-size strawberries, cleaned and cut up,
plus one for garnish
1 tsp. powdered sugar
1 oz. lime juice

Blend all ingredients with a cup of ice and strain
into medium-size wine glass. Garnish with the
fresh, whole strawberry.

Godfather (Scotch) or
Godmother (vodka)
1 oz. Scotch or vodka
1 oz. Amaretto

Pour over ice in a rocks glass.

Life is just a journey down a long path; just take the walk and enjoy all of what surrounds you. (Leslie—40)

¤

Never be bullied into silence, never allow yourself to be made a victim. Accept no one's definition of your life; define it yourself. (Bob—52)

¤

Always remember to make a wish every day. When you stop wishing, you'll feel a part of yourself cry. So, don't stop. (Sharon—32)

¤

Whatever choices you make in your life, remember, you own them! (Lois—39)

¤

Live simple and have simple problems. (Man—46)

Style on New Year's Eve

New Year's Shooter
⅓ oz. White rum
⅓ oz. Sambuca
⅓ oz. Triple Sec

Layer ingredients in a shot glass.

Ritz Fizz
1 sugar cube
3 dashes Angostura bitters
1 oz. brandy or cognac
Chilled champagne

Put the sugar in champagne flute and add bitters.
Add brandy then fill the glass with chilled
champagne. Stir gently.

Open to the wonder...and dance with the universe.
(Woman—46 years young)

¤

The key to life is how you handle Plan B.   (Frank—
62)

¤

Life is hard. Compared to what? (Nakia—26)

¤

Life is not one big party—it's a series of little
ones. Happy New Year. (Peter—61)

¤

You can sit in the bleachers and watch, or you can
be part of the game. You choose! (Man—39)

The Martini
Shaken or stirred...yes, it matters.

Dry Martini
1 2/3 oz. Gin
1/3 oz. dry vermouth

Stir vermouth and gin over ice cubes in mixing glass. Strain into cocktail glass. Serve with olive or a twist of lemon. The less vermouth you add, the drier your cocktail will be.

Dirty Martini
Dash of dry vermouth
3 oz. gin or vodka
$\frac{1}{4}$ oz. olive brine
Cocktail olive

Stir all ingredients with ice in a mixing glass. Strain into a chilled martini glass. Garnish with olive.

There's one thing I learned in the last year and that is, life is fun. (Jay—24)

⚥

In three words I can sum up everything I've learned about life: It goes on. (Bob—52)

⚥

Life is a wonderful thing. Embrace it and love all it has to offer—good and bad. Love the person you have in your life as you like to be loved. Take care of your children. It's not a job, but a gift. And love your neighbors even if they hate you.
(Cory—61)

⚥

It may be that your sole purpose in life is simply to serve as a warning to others. (Man—38)

Sour Apple Martini
2 oz. citrus vodka
½ oz. sour apple
½ oz. Triple Sec or Cointreau
¾ oz. fresh lemon juice
Thin slice of granny smith apple for garnish

Shake all ingredients with ice. Strain into chilled
martini glass and garnish with apple slice.

Apples and Oranges Martini
1 oz. apple liqueur
1 oz. cranberry juice
1½ oz. orange vodka
Orange peel for garnish
Thin slice of Granny Smith apple

Shake all ingredients with ice. Strain into chilled
martini glass. To garnish, squeeze the oil from the
orange peel over the top of the drink, discard the
peel and drop in the apple slice.

This was written in pencil on the black metal back seat of a bus in northern Thailand many, many years ago: "A man has not lived until he has almost died. For those who have fought, life has a flavor the protected will never know."
(A Vietnam Veteran—67)

¤

Death is what makes living an event. (Man—54)

¤

Do it now! I hear none of us are getting out of this alive. (Man—44)

¤

Hope for the best but expect the worst, and you will have few disappointments in life. (Dennis—52)

Rosy Martini
2 oz. citrus vodka
½ oz. Triple Sec
½ oz. Red Dubonnet
Flamed orange peel

Stir first three ingredients with ice and strain into a chilled martini glass. Garnish with flamed orange peel.

Smoky Martini
2½ oz. gin or vodka
Splash of blended Scotch
Lemon twist

Stir gin or vodka and Scotch with ice to chill. Strain into chilled martini glass. Garnish with lemon.

Life is like picking raspberries: You have to look at the plant in many angles to find all the fruit.
(Woman—54)

¤

Things' I've learned from life: Let only God judge you, for everyone else is certainly wrong. Yesterday is history; the future is now. You only need four hours of sleep a night. You're missing out on the entire ferry ride if you wait in your car the whole time. Nothing is impossible—just look at our president. We're all going to die sometime. It's our goal in life to have our memories live forever.
(Kyle—17)

¤

Life is too short, let it go. (Linda—48)

¤

The happiest of people don't necessarily have the best of everything; they just make the most of everything that comes their way. (Woman—52)

Upside-Down Martini
2½ oz. dry vermouth
1 oz. gin
Lemon peel

Stir vermouth and gin with ice. Strain into a chilled martini glass and garnish with the lemon peel.

Watermelon Martini
½ oz. fresh lemon juice
1 oz. Midori
1 oz. citrus vodka
1½ oz. fresh watermelon juice
Fresh mint leaf

Shake lemon juice, Midori, vodka, and watermelon juice with ice. Strain into a chilled martini glass. Garnish with mint.

Nobody really cares if you're miserable, so you might as well be happy. (Woman—42)

¤

What I know to be true is that I am 17 days short of being 39, feeling great with my best buddies, free for the day, happy 80 percent of the time. (Andrea—38)

¤

Happiness is different things for different people, for me it is to see his big smile, it fills my soul with joy. (Sue—35)

¤

We are ending our trip from New Hampshire and heading home, and the only philosophic thought I have is: If you wake up in the morning and you are not happy with your life, it's time to make a change! So, New Hampshire, here I come! (Woman—33)

Shooters

Beam Me Up, Scotty
$\frac{3}{4}$ oz. Kahlua
$\frac{3}{4}$ oz. Crème de Banana Liqueur
$\frac{1}{2}$ oz. Bailey's

Layer all ingredients in order above.

For each of the following recipes, shake ingredients with ice and strain into a shot glass.

B-51
$\frac{3}{4}$ oz. Kahlua
$\frac{3}{4}$ oz. Irish Crème
$\frac{1}{2}$ oz. 151 rum

B-52
$\frac{3}{4}$ oz. Kahlua
$\frac{3}{4}$ oz. Irish Crème
$\frac{3}{4}$ oz. Grand Marnier

Jelly Bean
$\frac{3}{4}$ oz. Anisette
$\frac{3}{4}$ oz. blackberry brandy

The real art of conversation is not only to say the right thing at the right place but to leave unsaid the wrong thing at the tempting moment.
(Woman—52)

¤

Nobody ever died of laughter. —Max Beerbohm

¤

What I know to be true is: Laughter does heal all woes; make someone guffaw and you're sure to do the same! (Nicole—32, loving my 30s more than my 20s because I still have fun, but I'm wiser and have the money to play with!)

¤

I intend to live forever—so far so good. (Man—38)

Beer is a liquor fermented from cereals and malt and flavored with hops.

There are over 17 million possible cocktail variations that can be made from the contents of a top-notch bar. So what are we waiting for?

There is nothing which has yet been contrived by man, by which so much happiness is produced as by a good tavern or inn.
—Samuel Johnson

Within our lives, we have surely crossed paths with men who were asked to give of themselves and at times pay the ultimate price so that others may be free...Remember these veterans, and pay homage to their deeds. They stand silent, and at times remember things that you and I may never wish to see. Be proud, and never take anything for granted. Your freedom was assured by their sacrifices. Next time you see a Vet, acknowledge them and thank them, even if with just a smile. (Man—34)

¤

By hook or by crook, we're the last to sign your book! (Nancy, 52, and Fred, 64)

¤

Last Orders Please!

Bourbon or Whiskey Highball
2 oz. bourbon or whiskey
Ginger ale or club soda

Fill highball glass with bourbon or whiskey, ginger ale or club soda, and ice cubes. Add twist of lemon peel, if desired. Stir.

Brandy Alexander
1 oz. cream
2 tsps. whipped cream
$\frac{3}{4}$ oz. dark Crème de Cacao
1 oz. brandy
Nutmeg

In a shaker, combine cream, whipped cream, crème de Cacao, and brandy. Shake well. Strain into cocktail glass and sprinkle with nutmeg.
$\frac{3}{4}$ oz. Amaretto
$\frac{3}{4}$ oz. sloe gin
Grenadine